GROWING IN THE GOSPELS

Faith and Academia

*The Search for the Original Meaning
of the Bible*

Michael Harvey Koplitz

Faith and Academia
The Search for the Original Meaning of the Bible

In 2009, John Crossan published his book "Jesus A Revolutionary Biography." Crosson is well known in the faith community for his academic work in Christianity. In this book, he has a chapter titled "Dogs under the Cross." After reading this chapter, I came to realize that there was a difference between reading the Bible as faith and reading it as academia. Let me tell you, I was 35 when I came to understand Jesus as the Messiah. I grew up in a non-practicing Jewish household. My paternal grandmother made sure that I and my older brother studied in the local synagogue and were bar-mitzvah. For Clara, it was unacceptable to have grandsons that did not follow Jewish practices. She knew her son and his wife would not engage in Judaism beyond Rosh Hashanah, Yom Kippur, and one seder on the Passover.

I want you to know this because it is important to understand that I do not have the paradigms that almost every Christian I have met has. A Christian who started attending church as a baby, was baptized, and sent to Sunday School was taught paradigms about the Bible and the faith that is deeply engraved on their souls. I must say I do not have this problem since I started attending church at 35 years old. It is important to understand that if one is going to introduce new ideas, that if the idea is against a paradigm, some negative feedback will occur.

Let me give you an example. Oh, but first I should tell you that after coming to an understanding of Jesus, I was called by him to preach the original meaning of the Bible. At 35 years old, I had not touched a Bible since I was 13 (that's Bar-Mitzvah age), and definitely not a New Testament. The paradigms from the church about the Bible were not burned into my soul. Perhaps that is why Jesus called me. The vision led me to ordained ministry, which involved earning a Master's in Divinity degree. I am an ordained Elder. I pastored churches for 25 years. Oh yeah, I have a Doctor of Ministry degree and am a Doctor of Philosophy. The D.Min. is in Christian leadership. The Ph.D is in Hebraic understandings in Christianity, the search for the original meaning of the Bible. Ever since I started seminary, I questioned everything.

I always tried to keep to my calling and learn the original meaning of the Bible. This was not a simple task, but I did it. Now you should know where I come from.

So, here is the first example. I attended a lay member led men's Bible study while at one church. I will not mention church names, and especially people's names, for obvious reasons. I was new to Bible study and thought Bible study meant that we could explore new ideas. One night, I attended the lesson and introduced different thoughts. The text the group was examining was the murder of Abel by Cain. Seems like a simple passage. Right? Actually, there are potential nuances to this story. The leader said that Cain killed Abel because the LORD rejected his offering. Yes, I agreed with that. But then he said that Cain was angry after the murder because the LORD rejected his offering. I then chimed in. How about the idea that after the murder, Cain became angry with himself because he knew what he had done was sinful? It is a fair question to ask. Wow, the leader's face turned red and his response was definitely not Christian. It turned out that his father was a Baptist preacher and how dare I question what his father taught him? I was not questioning it. I was offering alternative understandings. Isn't that what Bible study is all about? In that setting, it was not. I ran into the leader's unmovable paradigm.

Let me continue with Bible study by expanding it to Sunday School. I mean no offense to the multitude of volunteers who teach Sunday School. Every church I pastored had such a group of people. However, none of them had training. In fact, my home church would let anyone teach the lesson. The teacher would be given the teacher's guide with all the questions and answers, and they would offer the lesson in verbatim from the book. One church I pastored had a wonderful gentleman who ran his Sunday school class using a purchased curriculum. That's cool. Each book had 12 chapters. His class would run in 12-week cycles. He covered one chapter in the book every week. I sat in the class as the new pastor to get a feel of what was happening. He reminded me of my English literature professor in college. The class started with prayer. He then said "pull out your book and turn to page 35." He then read the questions that were at the end of the chapter he was on and gave the people the answer from his teacher's guide. So, stupid me asked about the answer. He felt dumbfounded when I asked about the book's answer. In his twenty-five years, that never happened to him. Well, because of my question, we never got through all the questions in the book. He said at the end of the class time that the class would move to the next chapter in the book next Sunday. Again, not being too smart, I asked why he would not continue in the chapter that we did not finish. I was strongly told that he did one chapter a Sunday, period!

He and his class learned whatever the author of the study believed and wrote. There was no room for any kind of discussion or expansion of knowledge. His understanding of Christian theology was extremely thin. When I said I would help him learn a more in-depth understanding of theology, he was quick to tell me he had been doing these studies, his way, for twenty-five years, and who did I think I was to offer a different way. Duh, I was ordained with a Master of Divinity degree. That's why. Then I backed off because he was not looking thrilled. Another paradigm.

I could easily continue with stories like these two. My guess is that you could easily do the same thing. I have also listened to preachers who do not have the faith or academics of the Bible correct. One lady named "the angel lady" said some very interesting things in a sermon about the Trinity. I cannot remember exactly what she said but I say that she was 100% incorrect. More than likely, most of the people in the pews did not know that she was presenting a heresy, according to the accepted church doctrine. This example, and there are plenty of others, shows that there are people out there preaching the Word of the LORD with no education and training. Therefore, they should not be expected to get it right. However, the congregations they are preaching to don't know that. From their point of view, the preaching is correct. People in the pews do not question what they hear. Perhaps it is unfortunate that I listen.

I have been in retirement for two years and can only listen to one preacher on Sunday. This person is my pastoral mentor. We have had conversations about faith and academia. He is very well educated in the faith, the Bible, doctrine, and most important he knows church and biblical history. If I disagree with something he said, I can converse with him about it. He wants me to bring any thoughts to him. So, there are at least two of us who love to engage in doctrinal, biblical theologies. He has been extremely helpful to me in my quest to understand the original meaning of the Bible. I can even surprise him now and then with discovered insights.

What does my quest to recover the original meaning of the Bible mean? When Jesus spoke, what did the people think he meant? Some readers will stop after this next point. The church has a lot of things wrong. Please don't stop reading. Let me explain why. The first question to you is which English Bible version are you using? It matters!!! The translation committee of your English Bible, apart from the King James and early English translations, has a preface describing their translation process. For example, the New International Version (NIV) translation committee stated that the translation was true to the original language, except where church tradition is strong.

What does that mean? Here is an example, Isaiah 7:14:

> [4] "Therefore the Lord Himself will give you a sign: Behold, a virgin will be with child and bear a son, and she will call His name Immanuel.

Sorry reader, this is a BAD translation. The Hebrew word in the verse is: עַלְמָה

This word means "young woman." It does not mean virgin. So, when people heard this verse originally read, they thought "the young woman will be with child and bear a son." This verse has nothing to do with Mary being a virgin. How did the church come to say something different, you may ask? The Bible the church used for centuries was the Vulgate. The

Vulgate is the Latin translation of the Bible. When the Vulgate was written the translator named Jerome made a few changes. For those who are unaware, the Vulgate is the Latin approved translation of the Bible. Saint Jerome did the translation under the order of the Pope around 350 CE. Jerome left notes of things he changed as he made his translation. Therefore, the Catholic church is based on a Bible that is actually partly commentary. The commentary is from Saint Jerome and he changed verses he did not agree with. The idea of Mary being a virgin is a foundation of the church by 350 CE and, yes, still today. Jerome had to change the Isaiah verse that the church was using as proof that Mary was a virgin. So, he changed it. Now you know where this translation came from. Please remember that I am not disputing whether Mary was a virgin. I have academically proved that Isaiah 7:14 is not a verse which proves the church's position. Oh yes, there are plenty more where this one came from.

Even my favorite English version, the New American Standard Bible 1995, has the wrong translation. The translation committee said they stuck to the original text. Obviously, they did not here. Why? In all honesty, publishers publish Bibles to make lots of money. After all, the Bible is a best seller. The publisher would lose sales if they correctly translated Isaiah 7:14 and other verses of the Bible. So, money is an issue here. That's not really a surprise.

So a lot of faith in the Christian religion is not biblically based. Rather, it is based on tradition. Wait, a moment. For those who are not Catholic, you need to know that the Catholic and Orthodox church base their faith doctrines on traditions. The virgin Mary from Isaiah 7:14 is one of them. Let me show you a bit of academia here. St. Augustine said that Satan was in the Garden of Eden and tricked

Eve. Please pull out any Bible you have and find this. You cannot! You might believe the serpent was Satan because the church told you so. That's what Augustine decided. He also added that children are created in sin. The "original sin" of Adam and Eve is passed down through the act of procreation. That's why Mary had to be a virgin so Jesus would not be born in sin. Oh yes, take it one step further because he also said that Anna, Mary's mother, was a virgin when Mary was born. You never heard this? That's because the Church banned the Gospel of Mary (not the Gnostic version). That book was supposed to be the first book of the New Testament until the Bishops in 456 CE decided to toss it. Did I just give another academia point? I did. People called Bishops determined what the Bible would contain. They selected the books of the Bible to match the traditions that had been established. Sounds backward, yes it does.

A fantastic book to read is the "Book of the Watchers" which is the first thirty-six pages of 1 Enoch. Many are thinking, what book is this? Your Sunday School teacher and probably pastor or preacher have no clue about this book. Jesus quotes it, approximately 1/3rd of Jude is directly from 1 Enoch. The reason you don't know about it is because around 600 CE the church banned it. The most read books in Jesus' day were Isaiah and 1 Enoch. Archeologists have discovered more copies of these two books at sites dating back to Jesus' day than any other books.

Do you believe Satan is a fallen angel from Heaven? Most Christians say "yes." Guess what? That is from the Book of the Watchers. You know a little about the Watchers from Genesis 6:1-6. They appear just before the Noah flood narrative. So, Satan cannot be in the Garden because Aziel, the fallen angel, has not fallen from Heaven yet. So, Augustine was wrong. But the church adopted his position and made it tradition. Today, almost every Christian denomination and group believe in the doctrine of Original Sin. Oh yes, the LORD said to Noah to repopulate the Earth. Why would the LORD tell us to commit a sin to have children? The church tradition of original sin just does not hold up when placed against academia. However, since those who attend church have had this tradition drilled into their brains, they will fight you even though the academic proof is airtight.

The church liked to burn the writings of any Christian expression that did not follow their traditions and doctrines. There were several expressions of Christianity after Jesus' ascension. Why? A simple answer is that Jesus did not tell us what everything meant, like communion and baptism. Jesus did not want a new religion. He wanted Judaism to reform. So, we must examine what happened when Christianity broke away from Judaism. We must move to academia for a little while. Grab onto something if you need to because the ride will get bumpy.

The remaining eleven disciples (remember that Judas Iscariot was dead) went out into the world to spread the Gospel. The Bible does not tell us of their successes or failures, except a little about Peter. There are books that do, but the church has banned them. There is a book called the "Acts of ____," where the blank is the name of each disciple. If we go to these banded from the Bible books, we are in pure academia mode. So, to stay balanced between faith and academia, we start with the book of Acts and move to the Pauline letters. Paul is the key to the breakup between Judaism and the emerging Christian movement.

At the beginning of the movement, the disciples of Jesus were just like the disciples of any rabbi. They wanted to know everything that

Jesus said and know why he did what he did. They wanted to emulate who he was. Jesus said that he came to fulfill the Torah and the prophets. Therefore, Jews could become disciples. There is a story in Acts of Peter's vision of animals. From the faith point of view, it says that Jesus told Peter that all food was now clean to eat. From an academic point of view, it is a story that allowed Paul's churches to not have to become Jewish to be followers of Jesus. How could Jesus say that Peter could ignore kosher laws when kosher laws are in Leviticus? Oops, that is a Torah book. Jesus cannot fulfill the Torah by throwing out one of the basic commandments in the Torah. The faithful say, "great, we can eat bacon." The academic study would show the problem with this narrative and place a large cloud of doubt over it.

Sometimes Christians forget that the people who wrote the Gospels and other writings in the New Testament did so years after Jesus' life. Many of the narratives would have been handed down mouth to ear. One of the earliest expressions of Christianity was the Proto-Orthodox church. This was Paul's invention. First thing you need to know is that the Proto-Orthodox church was not kind to other expressions of Christianity. If you don't agree with this statement, you can find the academic proof is in the Pauline letters. How many times did Paul say that he had the exclusive information and authority to decide what the church was to believe and practice? The churches that Paul created became the Proto-Orthodox church. This church destroyed all the writings they could find by other Christian expressions. Luckily for us, the Gnostics in northern Egypt placed copies of their writings into jars and buried them in the sands around Alexandria, Egypt. These documents were discovered in 1948. For those who wonder, that was the same year that the Dead Sea scrolls were found.

The Gnostic expression of Christianity differs greatly from what we have today. Now academia comes into play. In 2018, I was examining the origins of Communion, searching for the original meaning. I talked to a pastor in my Conference who had a PhD in theology and his dissertation was on Communion. I asked about Jesus saying that the wine represented his blood. That was a major problem for me to handle. Why do you ask? Leviticus strictly forbids the drinking of blood. Even Paul agreed to tell his new churches not to drink blood. The Nephilim (sometimes called the Giants) killed humans and drank their blood, which caused the LORD to address the Watchers' problem. This is from the Book of the Watchers.

So, drinking blood is out. Why would Jesus say, "drink my blood?" There is a cultural aspect to what the men around the table regarding what Jesus said. Let me give you this information first. When a rabbi was ready to "graduate" his class, he would take bread and wine and hold a ceremony that mimics the Last Supper. He would take the bread and tear off a piece and would say, "this is my body." When Jesus did this, his disciples knew he was asking them if they were ready and willing to become rabbis of his teachings. If they took the bread and ate it, they agreed to continue to follow his ways and teach others. Since Jesus knew he was about to die, he had to hold the ceremony. After three years, ready or not, his twelve disciples had to be ready. There was no other choice possible. Would they go out and make Jesus proud? Taking the bread and eating is equivalent to someone signing a contract.

Then he picked up the cup of wine and said, "This is my blood" and so on. This culturally meant that each person who agreed to become a teacher of Jesus' way needed to understand that it would not be easy, and they would probably die doing Jesus' work. This was a binding contract. Academically, Judas Iscariot took the oath and then broke it. In the Near East, an oath was binding. It is possible Judas hung himself because he knew he violated the oath. He might not have known that Jesus was going to have the ceremony. There he was, stuck. The other men would have known something was up if Judas refused the bread and wine. Of course, there is the possibility that the eleven disciples grabbed Judas and lynched him for violating his oath. Breaking of an oath was just not done without ramifications in those days.

Of course, the church decided that Judas Iscariot was a traitor, and it was his greed for money that allowed him to turn into Jesus. Academically, 30 pieces of silver is not very much money. A field worker got one silver coin for a day's work. Did Judas betray Jesus for a month's pay? It seems unlikely. Judas might have done it to spark the Passover riot and revolution, which happened almost every year after the Romans took over Judea. I sent this idea in a sermon message to a sermon website, a conservative one, and it was rejected. The response was almost longer than the sermon. The reviewer called it heresy to say that Judas was anything but a greedy traitor. So much for opening people's eyes to the original meaning of the Scripture. The reviewer's faith was in what the church traditionally has said for 2000 years. From his point of view, there is no other answer. That is one of the enormous problems. To venture outside the lanes of your church's theological position is considered heresy. It is not possible to grow when paradigms are held so tightly.

Back to Paul. He appeared to have some success convincing Jews that Jesus was the Messiah of the Torah and prophets. However, it was not enough of a conversion to keep the faith alive. Now, back to communion for a moment. The understanding that the Church today has of the purpose of communion comes from the Mithras Cult. About 90% of the doctrine of Christianity today comes from the Mithras religion. The foundational stone of Mithras is that Mithras died for the sins of his followers. Mithras followers said that they ate the actual body of Mithras and drank its actual blood. Of course, they did not. They used bread and wine. Wait a moment, sounds like church!

Even today, the Catholic and Orthodox churches will tell you that the bread and wine used for communion turn into the actual body and blood of Jesus. Some churches even have a special safe to hold the left-over communion elements. During the Middle Ages, the bread would be placed into a container and paraded through the town with the proclamation that Jesus had returned. In many churches today unused bread and wine have to be disposed of carefully. Sometimes it is the priest who gets a bread and wine lunch. It is considered a desecration to toss out the elements. Have you ever noticed the gold pan that is placed below the chin of the person receiving communion? That is so if it slips out of the mouth, it will not hit the floor. Sounds silly? Faith says that the wafer is Jesus' flesh, yes, the actual flesh. academia says it is simply a communion wafer that one could consider being symbolic of Jesus' flesh.

Jews would not fully accept the drinking of blood through wine and bread being the body. The PhD communion theologian said to me he did not care what the original meaning of communion was. He only cared about what it meant today. How can you hold communion and call it something that Jesus commands you to do when if you refuse to accept what he meant it to be? Again, church tradition came in. The church's paradigm about the meaning of Communion is not what Jesus meant when he did the ceremony with his disciples.

So, here's a kicker. Paul converted Mithras House churches into Jesus' House churches. 90% of the rituals came from Mithras. Oh yes, we know the first Proto-Orthodox churches were house churches. Paul had an easier time convincing Mithras House churches they were worshiping the wrong deity. He substituted Jesus for Mithras. The Father took the place of the Sun. The Spirit was the Spirit. But Paul did not have Torahs to leave behind. Nor could he alone have developed a new religion. He did not have the time. Academically, I will say that the Mithras House churches changed their allegiance to the "new" God, and Paul left them with the rituals they had. Paul made a few minor changes in sexuality laws from the Mithras religion.

If you examine the Gnostic Gospels, you will see a lot of similarity to the church's beliefs.

However, one big difference is that in the Gnostic Gospels, Jesus did not die for anyone's sins. Rather, Jesus died to bring us the lost secret work that Moses received on Mount Sinai. These secrets get a person into Heaven. Wait, a moment because Jesus gave us the secrets and they are in the Christian Gospels and the Gnostic Gospels. Ready? Here is comes: Love God and love neighbor. That is the ticket to get into heaven.

The Proto-Orthodox church destroyed the Gnostic and other expressions of Christianity because Paul told them to only believe his expression of Christianity, which he based on the Mithras cult. Try to find some of Paul's commands from his letters in the Gospel. If Jesus did not say or do it, should the church be doing it because Paul said so? The Proto-Orthodox church placed Paul into an apostle position because he founded these house churches and allowed them to keep their Mithras rituals with the substitution of Jesus for Mithras. The evidence is overwhelming!

Now for some brass tacks. I cannot go into a Christian church and say to them most of what I have discovered over the past twenty-five years of searching for the original meaning of Scripture. I will admit that like John Crosson, there are cultural points that I can say academically are correct, but from a faith point of view, I might not believe.

Now let us rock your world even more. I mentioned Crosson's book at the very beginning of this comparison. The chapter "Dogs under the Cross" is a fascinating examination of what happened to Jesus' body. Even Crosson said that he does not believe that it happened. However, he is 100% spot on with his analysis of the culture of that time. Jesus was crucified as a criminal and an enemy of the Roman Empire. Only the Romans could do an execution.

The means of execution was crucifixion. I know you are still with me. Don't stop reading now.

Death was not what the Jews feared. Rather, it was the desecration of the body. When a Jew dies, the body is to be buried within 24 hours unless the next day is the Sabbath or High Holy day (Rosh Hashanah or Yom Kippur) and the body must not be desecrated. Today that means no autopsy. Romans would not take the body down off the cross.

Instead, they let it rot. Eventually, the flesh-eating birds would eat the body, the ligaments and tendons would decay or be eaten. The body, in a few days, would fall off the cross. Then the body became food for dogs. Dogs can eat rancid meat and not become ill. People did not feed dogs in the Near East. Can you imagine a pack of dogs waiting under the three crosses, just waiting for the remaining rotten flesh to fall to the ground? That is what Crosson said happened to Jesus' body. Remember, he said by faith he does not believe this. Yes, this is still a difficult thing for me to write. However, it fits the situation.

The Joseph of Amarathia story gives a Semitic faith story. Culturally, you need to know that if a Jew owned a burial cave; it was only used for family. The minute Jesus' body was placed into Joseph's cave, his family could never use it again. The dead family member would be placed in the cave. After an amount of time had passed, the only thing left would be the bones. These bones were placed in a small box and the family determined what to do with it. Burial caves were very expensive. There were also a few caves that were available. Therefore, to give up one's burial cave was a huge financial burden. This does not mean that Jesus' body was placed in a cave. It raises the question of what happened to the body.

One side note about the crucifixion is that nails were not usually used.

Nails cost money. Usually, the wrists and ankles were attached to the wooden cross by rope. The narrative about the crucifixion could have collected nails along the way. Remember that someone transmitted orally the story for at least thirty years until Mark wrote it down. Semitic people loved to embellish stories. That was a culture item for them. Once it was recorded, it got set in stone. It is hard to embellish a written story. However, an oral story will get embellished and will change overtime. Did you ever play telephone as a kid?

Semitic followers of a rabbi who was beloved throughout his life would write stories about their rabbi. Many of the stories gave the rabbi divine powers. Did the rabbi have divine powers? No. It was the culture of Semitic people to elevate their rabbi by giving him divine powers. A great example comes from the Middle Ages. The rabbi Isaac Luria, known as the Ari (which means lion), is one founder of the Kabbalah (the mystical understanding of the Torah). The Ari lived in the 16th century as the Kabbalistic movement began in Spain and then moved to the Near East to a town named Safed, when the Jews were forced out of Spain in 1492.

Ari's followers wrote a book titled "The Tales of the Ari." It is a wonderful collection of stories about the exploits of the Ari. There are several stories in the book where the Ari does some things that only the divine could do. No, the Ari did not do those things. It was the love of Ari's disciples and their culture which created the book of Ari stories. The followers of Jesus would have written books like the Tales of the Ari. They are called Matthew, Mark, Luke and John. In the Tales of the Ari, some of the incredible stories are spiritual lessons. Semitic writers do not worry about details and the historical truth of a story. What matters most is the spiritual lesson of the story.

You probably know about a kid name David who was anointed to become the second king of Israel by a guy named Samuel. Sure, you know where I am going. Let us set the scene by imagining there were 10,000 Philistines on a hill. There were 10,000 Israelites on the opposite side. A battle was about to occur. Let us not forget that the 10,000 Philistines had iron armor, swords, and other killing devices. The 10,000 Israelites had two, yes, two sets of armor and swords.

King Saul and his son Jonathan have the armor. The rest had farming tools. It is easy to determine the victory, right? The story says a 13-year-old boy named David went to Saul and said he wanted to face Goliath the Giant. Neither set of armor fit David, so he walked out alone. Imagine the laughter on the Philistine side of the hill. David stepped up to a wadi (a Near East creek) and collected five small stones. With his slingshot, he moved toward the giant. You can almost hear the laughter.

The boy wound up and threw one stone. The Bible says that David hit Goliath between the eyes. The stone sank into his head and killed him. Down fell the giant. Really? The way Semitic stories are told, there are four layers of understanding called Pardes. I will not explain Pardes except to say that the first level is written in a manner that children would remember the story. The spiritual learning is the key to the story, not whether the battle went that way. Israel won the battle. How? We really do not know. The spiritual lesson is that anything is possible with the LORD's help. The LORD ensured Israel won. I do not know how it could happen, but it did. That is important. Christian fundamentalist says that you must read the Bible literally and their paradigm will tell you that David killed Goliath with one stone. Then you can surprise them with the question, "What did David pick up five stones if he was sure he would kill Goliath with his first shot?" They cannot answer that question. However, Midrash does. What is Midrash? Midrashim (the plural of Midrash) are rabbinical stories that fill in the biblical gaps. Midrash says that Goliath had four brothers who were his armor bearers. David was concerned that they would rush him. Therefore, he grabbed five stones.

Reading the Bible literally is a HUGE mistake! Semitic writers did not write literally. Everything was written with symbolism and allegories. What is worse is that when Christianity and Judaism separated, the Proto-Orthodox church used Greek philosophy to understand the Near East documents. Semitic people tell stories differently. They were not as concerned about the details. That is why we have four different stories about Jesus rising from the grave. Hold on, they are all the same story! To a Near Eastern storyteller, it does not matter who went to the cave, who got there first, or any of the details. The main thing is, does the reader understand Jesus rose from the dead just like he said he would? The rest is fluff or story line to tell the reader more about the spiritual aspects of Jesus' rising from the dead.

A difference between reading the Bible as a Greek philosopher and a Semitic philosopher is a literal view of the stories versus a spiritual awareness view. By the way, the Greek philosophy method started in Plato's academy and has been the way western civilization has developed. You and I learned the Greek philosophical methods while going through school. Again, let me repeat, the Bible is a Near Eastern document written by Semitic peoples in a Semitic way. If you are going to read the Bible and examine it using your Greek philosophical training, you will not find the original meaning of the Scripture.

It took me a while to stop reading the Bible through Greek philosophy. I had been trained in Seminary which teaches how the church requires the interpretation of Scripture to be done. That is a Greek way of reading it. Then I learned the Semitic way of reading the Bible. A whole new world opened up for me. I could imagine sitting on a stone and understanding every word Jesus said. I can hear the spiritual awareness in the Semitic stories. I value the different expressions of the same event. I appreciate the Semitic way of storytelling. I have discovered the original meaning of Scripture. I can hear and understand what the people heard and understood when Jesus spoke. This also includes the other speakers in the Bible. I understand where the Church of today has its traditions and doctrines. I can separate church doctrine to discover which is biblically based and which is not.

It was an exciting moment when it happened. This discovery has moved me into writing a lot. I have commentaries completed on the Gospels, Paul's letters, the Revelation, and a lot of books in the Hebrew Scriptures. These books are done from the Semitic, original meaning view of the text. I have written several pieces on Church doctrine and point out where the doctrine does not follow the original meaning of the Scripture.

I appreciate the faith people have in the LORD through the traditions of the Church. The conversion of the Mithras House churches into Jesus' House churches was a good thing that Paul did. Even though 90% of the rituals of the church are pagan in nature, at least Christianity is worshiping the true God, the maker of Heaven and Earth.

Abraham the Patriarch wanted to get the people of his time to worship the maker of Heaven and

Earth. He showed how the wood and stone idols were not gods. Paul was like Abraham in that he got the people of the Mithras House churches to understand that they were worshiping idols. He could get them to worship the God, maker of heaven and earth. Even though I now disagree with many church traditions and doctrines because they are from Mithras, I am thankful to Paul that he got the pagan churches to turn to the LORD.

After 2,000 years, I would not expect the Christian church to give up everything that came from Mithras. That would destroy the faith. To make some beliefs and traditions of the church work, the meaning and origin were changed. Remember that I told you that the PhD theologian did not care about the origins of communion or its original meaning? He was only concerned about what it meant today. Perhaps that is the way the Mithras based doctrines need to be addressed.

I have learned that it is near impossible to reprogram a Christian from a faith that was established by the Church that he or she has been attending for years. I hope to open their eyes to the original meaning of Scripture because the spiritual lessons are there and under a cover. When you can understand what Jesus meant when he said or did something, you will uncover a wealth of spiritual awareness.

My prayer is that this examination has touched the reader and will desire to discover the original meaning of Scripture. This will sound like an advertisement. My apologies. I have many books on this topic that you can read. I also have an extensive website of the research that I have done on different parts of the Bible as I search for the original meaning of Scripture. I offered the website works at no cost to anyone who wants to discover the original meaning of Scripture. May the

LORD bless you in your faith and love for Him.